D0461281

Cell Phones

Don McLeese

Rourke
Publishing LLC
Vero Beach, Florida 32964

www.rourkepublishing.com

PHOTO CREDITS: © Daniel St. Pierre: Title Page; © Inacio Pire: page 4 left; © JoLin: page 4 top right, 25, 44; © Danny Smith: page 4 middle right; © Margo Harrison: page 4 bottom right; © Perry Correll: page 5 top; © Douglas Freer: page 5 bottom; © Chris Hellyar: page 6; © Jeff R. Clow: page 7; © Alan Goulet: page 8; © ktasos: page 9 top; © Tomasz Pietryszek: page 9 bottom; © Joan Breault: page 10 (tower); © Wojtek Kryczka: page 11; © Ana Abejon: page 12; © Duncan Walker: page 13; © Ryan Burke: page 14 left; © Library of Congress: page 14, 15; © Ryasick: page 16; © Tammy Bryngelson: page 17; © Brian Sullivan: page 18; © Fleyeing: page 19 left; © Jasmin Awad: page 19 right; © Gabrielle Lechner: page 20; © Simon Smith: page 21, 24; © Milos Luzanin: page 22 left; © Jakub Semeniok: page 22 middle; © Murat Koc: page 22 right; © Thomas Mounsey: page 23; © Jamalludin: page 24 bottom; © M. Fawver: page 26; © Julián Rovagnati: page 27; © Fantatista: page 28; © Feng Yu: page 29; © Darren Baker: page 31; © Ahmet Mert Onengut: page 32; © Christopher O'Driscoll: page 32 bottom; © Christine Glade: page 33; © Max Blain: page 34; © Tomasz Trojanowski: page 35; © Anthony Berenyi: page 36; © Justin Horrocks: page 37; © Chris Schmidt: page 38; André Schäfer: page 40; © Rich Legg: page 41; © Izabela Haber: page 42; © Apple: page 43

Editor: Nancy Harris

Cover Design by Nicky Stratford, bdpublishing.com

Interior Design by Renee Brady

Library of Congress Cataloging-in-Publication Data

McLeese, Don.
  Cell phones / Donald McLeese.
    p. cm. -- (Let's explore technology communications)
  Includes index.
  ISBN 978-1-60472-328-1
  1. Cellular telephones--Juvenile literature. I. Title.
  TK6570.M6M385 2008
  621.3845'6--dc22
                           2008019700

Printed in the USA

CG/CG

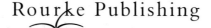

Rourke Publishing

www.rourkepublishing.com – rourke@rourkepublishing.com
Post Office Box 3328. Vero Beach. FL 32964

Contents

CHAPTER ONE

Cell Phones are Everywhere!

How many people do you know who have a **cell** phone? Do you have one? When you go to the store or the shopping mall, you'll probably see numerous people with cell phones at their ear, talking to family or friends. Cellular is the long word for cell. Sometimes, people call cell phones **mobile** phones.

As popular as cell phones are now, almost no one owned them until the 1990s. Prior to that, there had been some mobile phones that were attached to cars and only worked when you were in the car. The first mobile phone that you could carry around wasn't even invented until 1973, by a man named Martin Cooper who worked for a company called Motorola.

Cell phones have replaced most pay phones and phone booths.

The early cell phones were not similar to those used today. They were the size of a brick and too large to fit in your pocket or purse. They were much heavier than the ones we use now and very expensive. Only wealthy people or people who really needed them for their work owned them.

How would you like to carry one of these mobile phones in your pocket?

It wasn't until 1983 that a company called Ameritech started the first cell phone **network** in the United States. Even then, it was hard to imagine how many of us would have cell phones and how much we would come to rely on them!

CHAPTER TWO
Cellular Networks

Cellular describes the network of towers that divide a region into different areas called cells. If you are moving while talking on a cell phone, your call is passed from one cell tower to another.

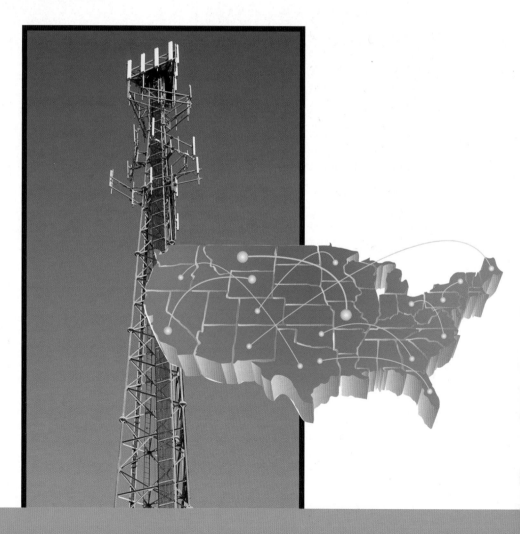

With the popularity of cell phones, you might wonder if truck drivers still use CB (citizens band) radios. The answer is yes! Most truck drivers do carry cell phones, but there are still many places along their routes with no cell service. Therefore, no truck driver should leave home without his CB radio. This important piccc of safety equipment works anywhere. And besides, talk is free on a CB!

Have you ever seen a honeycomb that bees make? A cellular system is like a big honeycomb, with each cell connected to the other by radio frequencies. A cell might be a mile or two in length or it might be many more miles.

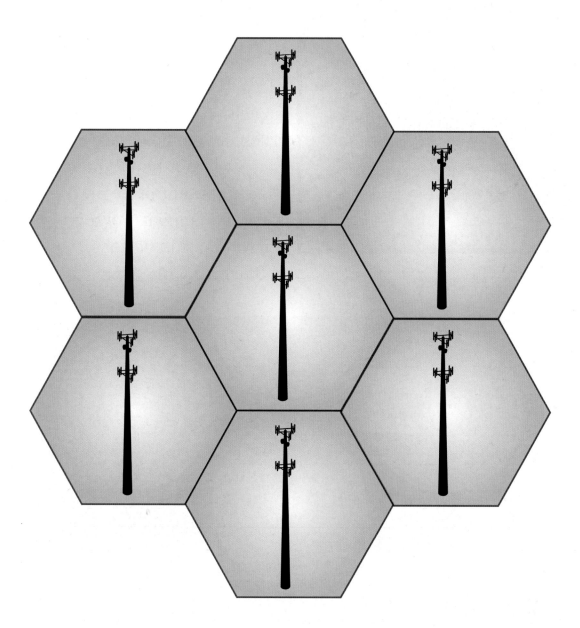

You never even know that your call is being switched from one cell phone tower to another! If you lose a call by passing out of a cell, we say that the call has been dropped. When you can't make or get calls on a cell phone, it is probably because you aren't within your cell phone's **service area**. This means you are too far away from a cell phone tower to receive service.

Cell Phone Towers

Cell phone towers may look like very tall poles, other towers have legs for support, and some are even designed to look like trees. Many of these towers provide service for several different cell phone companies.

CHAPTER THREE

Is It a Radio or Telephone?

Did you know that a cell phone is as similar to a small radio as it is to a telephone? The telephone was invented in 1876 by an American named Alexander Graham Bell. Until cell phones came along, all telephones required a series of wires for you to make a call. We call this type of phone a landline. Wires from a landline connect the telephone to a wall. Another wire outside of the wall connects the landline to a telephone pole.

Telephone poles are connected to one another by wires. In order for a landline to work, some part of the phone must be connected to the wires in the wall. If you don't have a portable phone, this makes it difficult if you want to walk around your house while talking on the phone.

In 1893, an inventor named Nikola Tesla showed how **wireless** communication worked, and this resulted in the development of radio. Instead of wires, the radio received signals through an **antenna**.

Nikola Tesla demonstrating how wireless radio communication works.

Nikola Tesla

In 1896, inventor Guglielmo Marconi became known as the inventor of the radio, after learning from and improving upon the experiments of Tesla and others.

Guglielmo Marconi

To operate cell phones, the cell phone tower works like a big radio antenna, sending and receiving signals. Your cell phone is as much like a radio as it is like a telephone. Since landlines are connected by wires, we often refer to cell phones as wireless phones.

Today, some people do not even have a phone at home connected through a landline. They only own a cell phone. Some other people who have both get service for their cell phone through the same company that provides their land line.

Pay Phones and Telephone Booths

Before cell phones became popular, if you were away from home and needed to make a call, you might have to find a pay phone. These were in stores, gas stations, and even along the sidewalks. Pay phones would often be inside a telephone booth where you could go inside and close the door so that other people couldn't hear your call. To pay for the call, you would use coins and insert them into the phone. Because so many people have cell phones, phone companies have removed the majority of their pay phones.

CHAPTER FOUR
Vibrations and Digits

In the past, when mobile phones were attached to cars, and very few people owned them, they used a system called **analog**. An analog system transforms a voice into electric vibrations or waves that are sent by a **transmitter** or tower and then picked up by an antenna.

Through the antenna, the vibrations are then turned back into a voice that the person receiving the call can hear. With an analog system, there aren't very many channels available to send and receive waves, so not many people in any area can use a mobile phone at the same time.

Today's cell phones use a **digital** system. Digits are numbers, and the numbers used in a digital system are 0 and 1. So instead of sending and receiving a sound as **waves**, or vibrations, a digital system turns those waves into numbers. It's like a code or language, that sends and receives sounds as a series of 0's and 1's.

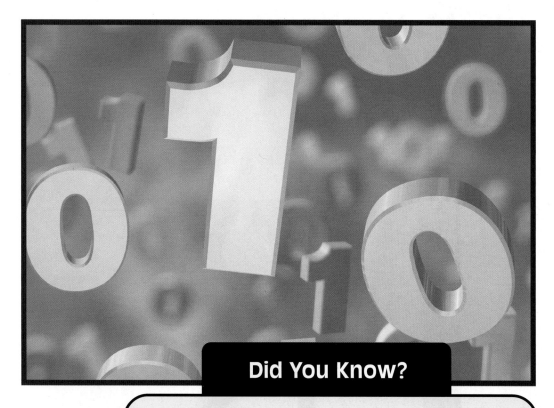

Did You Know?

It may be easy for you to pick up your cell phone and call a friend but it isn't easy for your cell phone. Your cell phone processes millions of calculations per second to keep your conversation going.

With a digital system, many more people in an area can use their phones at the same time than with an analog system.

Digital Computers

All computers speak the same digital language as cell phones. Advances in computers, as they've gotten smaller and more powerful, have allowed cell phones to do many more things than just send and receive calls. **Computer chips**, small pieces of silicon with electric circuits, have also gotten smaller, less expensive, and more powerful. They easily fit in cell phones. This allows cell phones to take photos and videos, send email, and connect to the Internet.

CHAPTER FIVE
Parts of a Cell phone

Every cell phone company produces different types of phones with different features. Customers choose the cell phone with the features, such as text messaging or GPS (Global Positioning System), that they will use.

All cell phones have many of the same parts. The circuit board inside of a cell phone has several computer chips and a microprocessor that allows you to send and receive calls.

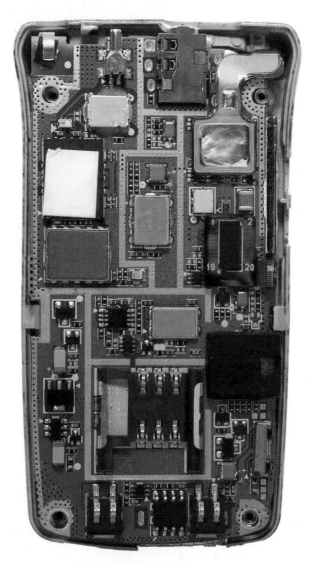

Inside of Cell Phone

Every cell phone has a subscriber identity module (SIM) card stored inside. It contains all of the personal identity information of the owner of the phone, such as the cell phone number, phone book, and text messages.

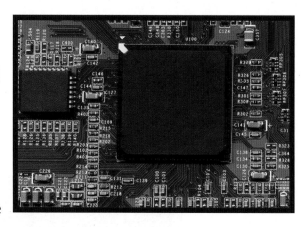

The screen on the front of a cell phone is called an **LCD**, or liquid display crystal. Below the LCD is the **keyboard**, with numbers or other figures on its various keys. On the keyboard, you press the phone number of the person you want to call. You speak into a **microphone** on your cell phone, and you hear through a **speaker**.

What gives your cell phone its power? A tiny **battery** provides the **electricity** to run it, so your phone doesn't need to be plugged into anything to work. When your battery is losing power, a special sound or a picture on your LCD alerts you. Then you can attach your cell phone to a charger that plugs into an electrical outlet, a car, or even a solar charger. After a few hours on the charger, your battery will have full power again.

Cell Phone Battery

Electric Battery Charger

CHAPTER SIX

More Than a Phone

How many things can a cell phone do? In the past, you could only do two things with a telephone: make calls or receive calls. But today's cell phones can perform many of the same tasks that a computer can.

Taking Picture with a Cell Phone

- Make sure there is plenty of light.
- Try not to take pictures of things with a bright light, or with the sun behind them.
- Take close-up pictures.
- Keep it still! Remember most camera phones have a delay between when you click the shutter to when the picture is taken.

Many phones have cameras in them. You can take and keep photos which can then be downloaded and printed. Some phones can even record and save videos!

Some phones let you store and listen to music, watch TV shows on the LCD, or connect to the Internet to check your email or surf the net.

Do you know why we call the keypad on this cell phone a QWERTY keypad? Its name comes from the first six letters on the left side of the keypad. English language computers and typewriters also use the QWERTY layout on their keyboards.

Many people, like you and your friends, use their cell phones even more for sending and receiving text messages than they do for making and answering calls. They call it **texting**.

What Does That Mean?	
G	Giggle or grin
?4U	I have a question for you
2MI	Too much information
LOL	Laugh out loud or lots of love
B4N	Bye for now
BFF	Best friends forever
PLZ	Please
SUP	What's up?

When you decide to switch companies and get your cell phone service from another cell company, you can choose to keep your same number but you will have to buy a new phone.

There are differences in networks from country to country. In order to make cell phone calls in a foreign country using your cell phone, you must make sure it is adapted for that purpose.

CHAPTER SEVEN
Cell Phone Do's and Don'ts

Do you know the word etiquette? It means the rules for being polite. Since cell phones have become so popular, we need to be especially careful to use cell phone etiquette, to insure that we aren't disturbing other people when we're using a cell phone.

Don't Talk and Drive

In California, Connecticut, Washington D.C., New Jersey, and New York, drivers must use a hands-free device, such as a Bluetooth or earpiece, with their cell phone when they are driving.

DON'T bother other people with your calls. Either leave and go somewhere private, or keep your voice down. Be careful when using a cell phone in public places such as restaurants and stores. Not only could you bother other people, but others might hear your personal conversation.

DO turn off your cell phone, or at least turn off the ring, in movie theaters, libraries, or other places where people expect it to be quiet.

DON'T ever use a cell phone in class, either to talk or to text. You need to pay attention to your teacher, not your cell phone!

DON'T use your cell phone to take pictures or videos of people who don't want their picture taken or who don't know that their picture is being taken.

DO be sure to understand your cell phone plan and what it charges in fees. There can be a charge for every time you make or get a call, every minute you spend on the phone, and every text message you send or receive. It all depends on the company that your family uses for cell phone service and the monthly plan that you have.

DO be particularly careful about **roaming** charges. Sometimes when you leave your company's service area, your call may be passed along to another company's tower. If this happens, the call might cost a lot more money.

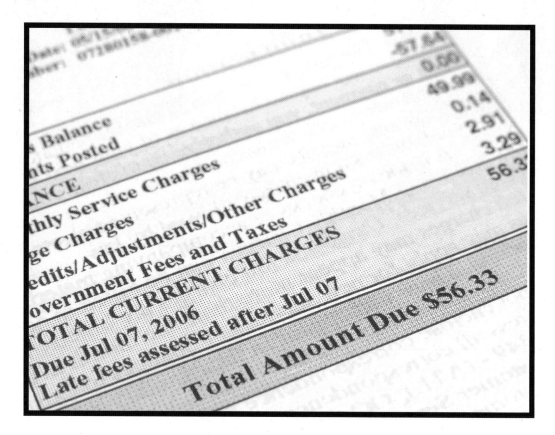

If you ever have any questions about using a cell phone, do ask an adult.

CHAPTER EIGHT
Turn It Off!

Have you ever seen a sign in a doctor's office or a hospital saying no cell phones can be used there? There are many places where cell phones don't belong, including, government offices, schools and library's. Please be respectful of this.

If you've been on an airplane, have you heard the flight attendant announce that all cell phones must be turned off before takeoff? Have you ever wondered why?

The signals sent by a cell phone to a tower can make the computerized machines used by doctors to stop working properly. Cell phone signals can also interfere with an airplane's computer system, which could cause serious problems.

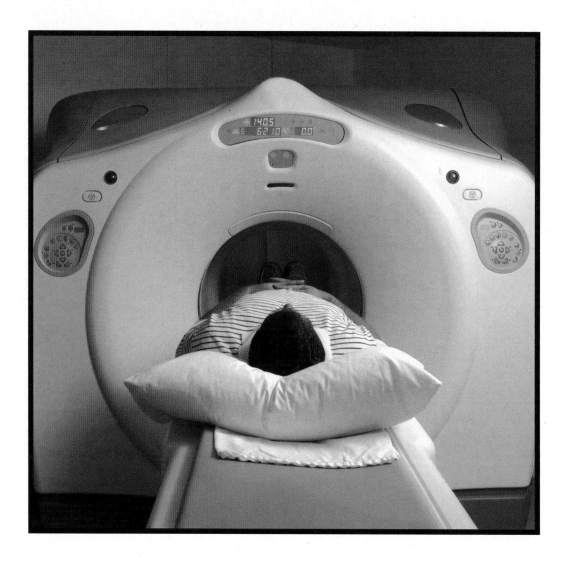

You should never have your cell phone turned on at the doctor's office or a hospital where a sign says cell phone use is forbidden.

You might be surprised the next time you fly if an announcement comes on saying that it's o.k. to use your cell phone to connect to the internet and check emails during the flight. But, before you decide to get connected, you might want to find out how much it will cost you. It could be expensive.

CHAPTER NINE

The Future of Cell Phones

As recently as the 1980s, it was hard to imagine how many people would own cell phones today and how many functions these phones would be able to perform. Now so many people have gotten accustomed to cell phones that it's hard to imagine life without them.

Cell phones have quickly changed the way we live our lives. Already, they help us stay connected to our friends and family, entertain us with games and videos, and help us find our way when we are lost. At some point, landlines might not exist at all. What will the cell phone do next?

Timeline

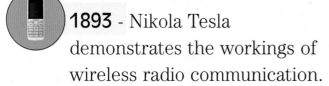 **1876** - Alexander Graham Bell invents the telephone.

  **1893** - Nikola Tesla demonstrates the workings of wireless radio communication.

 1896 - Guglielmo Marconi invents the radio.

1973 - Combining telephone and radio technology, Motorola's Martin Cooper invents the first mobile phone that you can carry around.

 1983 - The Ameritech company starts the first cell phone network in the United States.

 1990s - Cell phones start to get smaller and more popular, using digital technology.

Glossary

analog (AN-uh-log): a system that uses electric vibrations or waves rather than numbers to send information

antenna (an-TEN-uh): the part of the cell phone or cell phone tower that sends and receives the signals for a call

battery (BAT- uh -ree): the part inside the cell phone that provides the electricity that powers it

cell (SEL): each of the parts that are connected within a cellular system and are often similar in size and shape

cellular (SEL-yuh- lur): a system using cells

circuit board (SUR-kit BORD): the part inside of the cell phone that allows it to send and receive calls and text messages

computer chip (khum-PYOO-tur CHIP): a very small piece of silicon with electric circuits installed on it

digital (DIJ-uh-tuhl): a system that uses the digits 0 and 1 to perform tasks

electricity (i-lek-TRISS-uh-tee): a current of energy caused by the movement of electrons

email (EE-mayl): short for electronic mail, sent over the Internet by one computer user to another

keyboard (KEE-bord): the part of the cell phone beneath the LCD screen where you can press numbers (or letters for text messaging)

LCD (EL SEE DEE): short for liquid display crystal, the screen on a cell phone

microprocessor (MYE-kroh-PROSS-sess-ur): a very small chip that is the main part of the circuit board and processes all signals

mobile (MOH-buhl): having the ability to move

service area (SUR-viss AIR-ee-uh): the area where you can send and receive calls though your cell phone company

texting (TEXT-ing): sending text messages over cell phones

transmitter (transs-MIT-ur): a tower or a smaller device that sends a signal to be received

waves (WAYVS): energy vibrations that move or are sent through the air

website (WEB-site): a central location for related web pages on the Internet

wireless (WIRE-less): the ability of cell phones to communicate or computers to connect to the Internet without using wires or plugs

Index

Further reading

O'Connell, Jen. *The Cell Phone Decoder Ring*. Voice of Wireless, 2007.

Stetz, Penelope. *The Cell Phone Handbook*. FindTech Ltd., 2006.

Thompson, Henrietta. *Phone Book: The Ultimate Guide to the Cell Phone Phenomenon*. Thames and Hudson, 2005.

Websites

www.fcc.gov/cgb/kidszone/faqs_cellphones.html

www.keepkidshealthy.com/parenting_matters/
cell_phones_kids.html

www.://ezinearticles.com/?Kids-and-Cell-
Phones&id=1037

About the Author

Don McLeese is a journalism professor at the University of Iowa. He has written many articles for newspapers and magazines and many books for young students as well.